The Mermaid Legends

Poems for Children and the Young at Heart

JAMES WHITMER

The Mermaid Legends
POEMS FOR CHILDREN AND THE YOUNG AT HEART

iUniverse books may be ordered through booksellers or by contacting:

iUniverse
1663 Liberty Drive
Bloomington, IN 47403
www.iuniverse.com
844-349-9409

Because of the dynamic nature of the Internet, any web addresses or links contained in this book may have changed since publication and may no longer be valid. The views expressed in this work are solely those of the author and do not necessarily reflect the views of the publisher, and the publisher hereby disclaims any responsibility for them.

Any people depicted in stock imagery provided by Getty Images are models, and such images are being used for illustrative purposes only. Certain stock imagery © Getty Images.

ISBN: 978-1-6632-5021-6 (sc)
ISBN: 978-1-6632-5022-3 (e)

Library of Congress Control Number: 2023901687

Print information available on the last page.

iUniverse rev. date: 01/28/2023

Table of Contents

The Mermaid Legends

Book #1: *The Beginning*

The Red Octopus

His tentacles were dark as blood,
his eyes a ruby red.
A crimson wedge just like a star,
he wore upon his head.

Around his waist his thickened skin,
as red as Georgia clay,
matched the embers in his eyes,
deep red, or so they say.

He scanned the waters day and night,
always on alert.
He made the oceans safe and sound,
for minnows, squids, and squirts,
for starfish, crabs, and lobsters red,
for oysters in their shells,
for porpoises and dolphins gray,

as sailors rang their bells.

His burning eyes, like lava red,
glowed bright throughout the day,
guiding fish in thickened shoals,
pointing out the way.

He schools the mermaids young and old,
to aid those in distress,
to rescue sailors lost at sea,
to scan the waters without rest,
through darkest nights and waters deep,
through caverns where the starfish sleep.

In darkened waters ever deep,
this octopus of deepest red,
keeps his vigil without sleep,
protecting all, or so it's said.

The Mermaids

In the oceans far and deep,
the octopus, its vigil keeps,
among the mermaids and the fishes,
attentive to the mermaids' wishes.

They sit among the coral, white,
these mermaids with their eyes so bright,
whispering softly, listening low,
the stories being slowly told.

The octopus, his eyes deep red,
red as sunsets shining bright,
recites the legends he has known,
throughout the day, into the night.

Silently in waters blue,
fins like sparkling yellow sapphires,
glow and glisten as they listen,
eyes aglow, filled with desire.

This octopus, his tales renown,
his eyes as bright as jeweled crowns,
his tentacles bright as the sea,
they hold the lock. He holds the key.
The tales he spins soothe and amaze,
bring tears to open golden eyes,
then birthing smiles from deep red lips,
their mirthful faces can't disguise.

The Yellow Moon and the Golden Lagoon

Like golden lanterns in the night,
her eyes shone softly on the water.
The yellow moon above her bright,
her sailor lover, anxious, sought her.

His ship was moored a mile away,
through forests deep and rivers wide,
and through the darkness of the night,
those golden lanterns were his guide.

He found her sitting, calm, serene,
along a beach with waves of green,
and gentle, gray-white, frothy foam,
at a place she called her home.

These golden waters sparkled bright,
the calm lagoon a wondrous sight,
her mermaid eyes, his tilted cap,
a golden harp upon her lap.

The Squid with the Golden Harp

Old Sailors say from the watery depths
sweet voices of mermaids are heard.
When rounding the cape, their voices escape,
gently like wings of a bird.

And some folks say this music divine,
comes naught from the mouths of the maids,
but comes from the deep,
under waves fast and steep,
from a bright, golden harp being played.

But some sailors say this bright harp of gold
is played by a creature of red,
his singing quite long,
as he breaks out in song,
a bright crimson glow to his head.

But some folks say it's a mermaid's song,
from the dark, hollow depths of the deep,
but the old sailors know,
as the melody goes,
it wakes them up fast from their sleep.

But some folks say when the mermaids chant
and their whispers bubble up from the deep,
that a stiff chill fills their hearts and souls
like cold rain, hail, and sleet.

But old sailors know, this music sublime,
it comes from a bright harp of gold,
from a squid deeply red,
a bright glow to his head,
that only the mermaids have known.

BOOK 2: *The Mermaids*

Trebilina – The Mermaid with the Golden Eyes

Upon a lonely, lovely beach,
ivory white and pebbled thin,
a mermaid seeks her sailor love,
with golden eyes that match her fins.

Her golden tail, dangling free,
upon a rock near blue-green caves,
horizons deep and sunsets past,
cast their glow across the waves.

The sea breeze and the ocean sounds,
the gently flowing green-gray tides,
splash kisses on her golden tail,
golden tears in golden eyes.

Then suddenly a speck appears
across the gray-blue ocean line.

She breathes a heavy, heart-felt sigh,
gone golden tears from golden eyes.

She sees the topsails, then the rails,
sprinkled neat across the line,
separating moon from sea,
in silken, spider web design.

Silver-coated are the stars,
sparkling in the velvet night,
like *Trebilina's* deep-set stare,
as his ship comes into sight.

In the crow's nest high above,
she sees her long-lost sailor love.
He waves his red cap, seaman-like,
and blows a kiss into the night.

The Mermaid *Catalina* and the Swirling Tides

She waits among the swirling tides,
among the rushes and the reeds,
searching long across the line,
among the green-gray floating weeds.

That lonesome, solitary line
that separates blue sea from sun,
seems endless in its dark design,
and seeks to keep her love undone.

The ship she seeks, her namesake clear,
across the bow in letters bold,

is written neat and seaman-like,
Catalina, in sparkling gold.

And then as sunset, violet, deep,
makes its forlorn presence known,
a ship appears, its bow replete
with sparkling letters, all in gold.

She sees her name, breathes ever fast,
holds her breast, and prays at last,
and then she sees in letters bright,
Catalina, a wondrous sight.

The Mermaid *Sephora* and The Look-Out

Green feathers trimmed by yellow beads,
upon a wizened brow,
eyes that look straight out to sea,
across a weathered bow.

A sea of pearl smoothly set,
a whitecap not in sight,
the Look-Out's gaze is neatly met
by seabirds full in flight.

Distant lights among the mist,
a distant shore appeared.
A haven for a weary ship,
the shoreline slowly neared.

Upon the pier a shout arose,
from mothers, wives, and friends.

The wayward journey of the crew
was soon to find its end.

The lines flung out to welcome hands,
the anchor readied, taut.
The pilings sunk into the sands,
and lashed where ropes were caught.

The steady ship, its sojourn made,
gently heaved toward aft,
as swabbies from the seven seas
departed her at last.

And on this distant foggy shore,
the mermaid named *Sephora* waits,
her sailor lover soon to meet,
love in her heart he will create.

The Mermaid *Adriana* and the Castle at Night

Her eyes like sparkling jeweled gems,
she waits below the castle high,
its towers stretching endlessly
into the deep, dark, violet sky.

She sees him on the balcony
looking out to lonesome seas.
She prays he's longing for her touch,
a gentle kiss, her only plea.

On the sea ledge where she waits,
splashed by foaming blue-gray waves,

the sounds of music fill the night,
from high above into the caves.

Theses caves with seaweed and with foam,
from ocean waves and drifting tides,
echo melodies she seeks,
from where her sailor love resides.

And up above her in the mist,
his eyes meet hers, as tears are shed,
and through the starry night a kiss,
is blown with lovestruck words unsaid.

The Mermaid *Florina* and the Golden Crown

The golden crown *Florina* sought
was hidden deep in darkened caves,
below the silent depths of blue,
below the place where coral grew,
below the sleepy, rolling waves.

This golden crown bejeweled with gems
of sparkling sapphires, icy blue,
and rubies red as large as suns,
waits patiently like feet of nuns,
praying rosaries in the pews.

After dreary days of searching,
Florina found a crevice low.
Neat but narrow, coral grew there,
as white as freshly fallen snow.

And through this crevice dark and deep,
past jutting rocks like tiny islands,
all alone, she saw it glistening,
glowing bright, like sparkling diamonds.

And around this crown for kings,
a brightly colored eel sings.
In the deep and hollow depths,
he glows, he glistens, begs her steps
to come and take this jeweled crown,
releasing him, his duty done.

This single, solitary maid,
her eyes a deepened seaweed green,
retrieved the long-lost, jeweled crown,
swam through the crevice, upward bound.

The Mermaid *Gloriana* and the Midnight Watch

The ship makes ready in the night.
The moon above is shining bright.
Her sailor love on midnight watch
listens low, a pink-white conch,
clutched to his ear, her song to hear,
seeks out her splashes ever near.

In the glistening of the moon
she sings her lovely mermaid song.
Her heart is beating with the rhythm
of the waves that linger long.

He hears her mermaid melody,
whispers long her maiden name.
Gloriana does resound,
across the mizzenmast and frame,
across the topsail and the bow,

just like a sailor's solemn vow.

Its flags unfurled, her lover's ship
slowly moves away from shore,
making way among the waves,
her sailor lover gone once more.

Before she sheds a heartfelt tear,
he throws his conch into the sea.
With outstretched arms she captures it,
to her ear she hears his plea.

Inside this conch from ancient seas
she finds a sparkling, golden ring.
She then looks up and sees his ship,
into the night, away it slips,
while to the pink-white conch she clings.

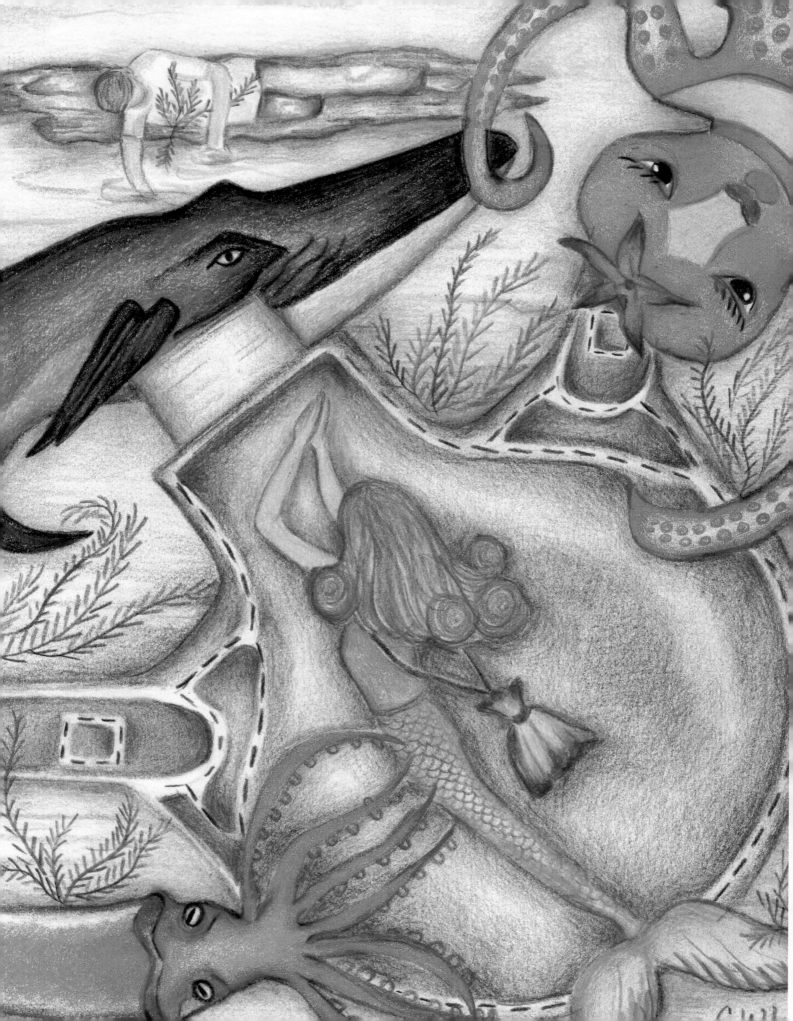

The Mermaid *Oriana* and the Blue-Black Whale

On a plank of hardened wood,
floating on a placid sea,
she saw a form stretched out across
its top, an arm, and then a knee.

She swam to where it floated free,
bobbing up and down,
and reached across his tattered shirt,
covered deep with seaweed, brown.

His lips were parched and black like eels.
His eyes were deeply shut.
His cheeks were hollow, gaunt, and grim.
He did not feel her touch.

She reached into her mermaid pouch,
retrieved a flask of water,
and gently dabbed it on his lips,
just like the octopus had taught her.

And then a drop on tired eyes,
then followed by another,
this sailor lost, woke from his sleep,
clutched her hands and smiled deep,
and on his face a brightened color.

Oriana scanned the sea,
calling out her mermaid song.
A blue-black whale then soon appeared,
its slashing tail thick and long.

Upon its back she strapped the sailor,
flush and fashioned tight.
Using seaweed dark and green,
and helped by squids throughout the night,
her eyes glowed with a velvet sheen,
yearning for the morning light.

She whispered in the whale's ear,
the night deep dark, the shoreline near,
and through the murky depths they sailed,
the wind, the waves, the squids did trail,

the blue-black whale's dark slashing tail.

In the darkness, deep but clear,
the shoreline coming into sight,
she held the sailor to her breast,
throughout the dark and gloomy night.

As they neared a shoreline bright
with lanterns glowing in the night,
she slowly bid the whale goodbye,
the squids now lost in full-flung flight,
the sailor's hands in hers held tight.

Upon her back and holding tight,
a long-lost sailor soon in sight,
she swam up to a lantern bright.
Within a lifeboat sailors rowed,
tossing out a vest of gold.

And to this vest he soon was held,
then hoisted to the safety of
his comrades as the blue sea swelled,
deep, dark the night, no stars above.

She swam away into the night,
a flickering glow upon the shore,
wondering if this sailor lost
would look upon her evermore.

Then at the point where sea meets moon,
she paused and saw this sailor swoon.
In a boat the sailor sat,
his hardened face, it seemed to be,
a look of forlorn love it held,
as desperate as the rolling sea.

Oriana, smiling softly,
in a calm but flowing sea,
slowly swam to far off waves,
wishing for that forlorn love,
and hoping it was she.

The Mermaid *Princess Zoe* and the Pearl Necklace

Upon her neck it sparkled bright,
in the dwindling evening's light,
a wondrous, glowing lustrous sight,
shiny pearls, her breath held tight.

Zoe knew from where it came.
All the mermaids knew her fame,
but on her princess mermaid neck,
this precious necklace did remain,
a princess with her eyes aflame.

Lost at sea for years and years,
this necklace sparkling bright,
was found within a cavern deep,
in hollow seas and lost from sight.

She wore it round her princess neck,
a talisman of sorts.
The other mermaids envied her,

the necklace bright as sparkling quartz.

But in the end the truth won out,
for *Zoe* truly knew,
to where this necklace should reside,
and so she acted tried and true.

To the princess high above
is where the necklace soon was flung,
with sympathy and long-lost love,
it landed flush on slippered feet,
a gleaming smile, their eyes did meet.

And on this jutting balcony
above a placid green-blue sea,
this tiny maiden, princess-like,
held the necklace, then with glee,
blew back a kiss for all to see.

The Maiden of the Mist – The Mermaid *Fianna*

She dwelled along the misty shores,
where waterfalls abound.
The sailors from the seven seas
knew that's where she'd be found.

They knew her name.
They knew her fame,
but dared not seek her out.
She loved but one, a sailor lost,
a love complete, a love devout,
and so she lonely, lingers long,
among the coral and the reefs,
her heart a puzzle to be solved,
her tears replete with solemn grief.

Her sailor love was lost at sea,
a tempest in the dead of night.
In rolling, rocking seas of dread,
the villain robbed her of her knight.

So now she waits among the mist,
among the rushes and the reeds.
Her pink-white conch still holds his kiss,
her hope a fleeting, desperate plea.

She yearns to hear her maiden name,
called from the crow's nest ever high.
To her ear her conch held soft,
the silence close and ever nigh.
His voice a silent memory,
the rolling tides and rocking waves,
the swirling winds and sea sounds swell,
inside the conch, his kiss remains.

From violet night to sundrenched morn,
she waits among the gray-white mist,
her sailor lover soon to come,
upon her conch to place his kiss,
the words *Fianna* whispered softly,
her eyes now filled with love and bliss.

The Mermaid *Lauriana* and the Conch with the Yellow Pearls

The pearls matched her golden hair,
sparkling in the dead of night.
Her eyes as bright as mornings blessed,
to her breast, the pearls held tight,
in a conch that matched her earrings,
brightly colored, pink and white.

Lauriana was her name.
All the sailors knew her fame.
Of the mermaids, sleek and slim,
Lauriana could outswim,

all the others, night and day,
diving deep and far away.

It was there she found the pearls,
nestled deep among the coral.
Gold-white coral, the legend tells,
with yellow pearls inside conch shells.

These same said pearls, beaded fine,
now rest across her neck sublime,
and sparkling deep into the night,
are *Lauriana's* guiding light.

CWL

The Mermaid *Bluebell*

Among the coral deep and blue,
where the starfish linger still,
Bluebell swims a figure-eight
that marks the years, a time until,
the clipper ship from far off lands
will return her sailor love,
along horizons deep with stars,
twinkling in the night above.

Her eyes are blue and crystal-like,
the color of a topaz bright.
Sailors say these searching eyes
are blue as sapphires, like the sky.

She swims her figure-eight each day,
until the year has passed away.

Eight long years she holds her tears,
waiting for that fateful day.

With tail fins deeply velvet blue,
sailors say like amethysts,
they sparkle with an orchid's hue,
like her lover's gentle kiss.
They sparkle in the mid-morn sun,
as the figure-eight is done.

It is then, among the coral,
as blue as any ocean deep,
she nestles low and listens for,
among the waters fast and steep,
the Look-Out's call for all to hear,
the words, "*Land ho*!" Her heart does seek.

The Mermaid *Cassia* and the Red Dolphin

Cassia, Cassia, the dolphins whisper,
but only one is red as fire,
and only one will *Cassia* follow,
her broken heart filled with desire.

This dolphin red, with eyes that sparkle
in the night, like burning embers,
leads the way through hollow caverns
to a place that he remembers.

Through deep, dark seas, through turns and
patterns,
he guides sweet *Cassia.* His back she rides,
through darkened seas and seaweed thick,
through waves that splash from side to side.

It is there in thickened sand,
rests the ship she longs to find,
among the seaweed and the coral,
and where her love is so confined.

To the hollow hulk he takes her,
riding on his crimson back.
Soon inside, he flips his tail,
and opens up the safe at last.

Into this coal-black safe she reaches
past the bars and rusted rails,
into the dungeon where it rests,
retrieves the locket, gold as moonlight,
around her neck it forms a crest.

Then to the surface like a whirlwind,
his eyes as red as glowing torches,
he whispers sweet her maiden name,
Cassia, with love that scorches.

As the locket opens slowly,
printed is her name in gold,
just above her sailor love's
picture, to her breast she holds.

The Mermaid *Graciella* and the Dancing Red Flamingo

In a place with shallow waters,
a place replete with dragonflies,
starfish wash upon the shoreline,
deeply blue the placid skies.

It is where flamingos dance,
their colors brightly pink and red.
Their beaks are shaped like sailors' hooks,
deep dark and black, or so it's said.

Graciella knows this place,
visits often, lingers long,
and with her emerald tail swishing,
she whispers out her maiden song.

But only one flamingo listens,
her long legs in the shining sun,
and on one leg she stands before her,
her dance, flamingo-like, begun.

All the others wander far,
among the rushes and the reeds,
but the dancing red flamingo,
completes her dance among the weeds.

With eyes that shine with dainty colors,
glowing like none of the others,
in the mid-morn sparkling sun,
she smiles and curtsies when she's done.

The Mermaid *Dolcina* and the Seahorse with the Silver Eyes

Sailors from horizons past
have searched and searched the oceans deep,
among the waves and flowing tides,
among the sea swells, swirling, steep.

They seek a seahorse, legends tell,
with silver eyes as bright as diamonds.
She dwells among the caverns deep,
among the many thousand islands.

Upon her face, no sailor looked.
Into her eyes, no sailor glanced.
Dolcina, only, knows the treasure,
has seen those eyes, as they have danced.

Eyes like lightening without thunder,
glow and sparkle, flashing brightly,
make *Dolcina* stop and wonder,
as she whispers soft and lightly,
at their beauty, eyes of midnight
glowing with soft, wondrous light.

Along a beach no sailor's seen,
among the turquoise coral deep,
along a shoreline in between,
the cattails where the starfish sleep,
this seahorse with bright silver eyes
returns to waters cold and steep,
her eyes like torches, glowing, flashing,
and where she was, the waves come crashing.

The Mermaid *Daviana* and the Golden Coral

In deep blue waters seldom seen,
except by whales of ocean green,
the rainbow fish with yellow tails,
swishing in the breeze like sails,
guard the coral bright as gold
in waters crystal clear but cold.

These rainbow fish, their colors bright,
at sunset glow like stars as bright
as any diamond in the sky,
and seen by sailors passing by.

But in the crystal, clear, cold water,
underneath from where they dance,
no sailor ventures, takes no chance,
because the waters where the coral,
as gold as any monarch's crown,
will suck them down beneath the surface,
and nevermore will they be found.

But *Daviana* knows the waters,
calls calmly to the rainbow fish,
and with their swishing golden tails,
a pathway to the coral exists.

Daviana dives in rhythm,
with the passage opened deep,
finds the coral growing brightly.
Yellow diamonds, they do keep.

Upward bound she swims to moonlight
glowing on the water's waves,
a bead of yellow diamonds glowing
like torches deep in darkened caves.

Resting neatly 'round her neck,
these beads do dazzle, hypnotize.
Swimming to the far horizon,
she holds her breath, holds tight her prize.

The Mermaid *Katiana* and the End of the Rainbow

Legends tell of starfish swimming
in thickened shoals, in waters deep,
and underneath their graceful movements,
is buried treasure where sea snakes sleep.

Sailors know not all the legend,
of rainbows vibrant they know not.
But *Katiana* knows the legend,
of rainbows ending, and the spot.

The starfish tell her how to get there,
and where the treasure rests in wait.
They tell her of the path to follow,
the rainbow like a swinging gate.

And when she finds that rainbowed gate,
guarded by green-gray sea snakes,
its lock is opened by their tails,
the treasure chest lashed down by stakes,

into the sandy ocean bottom,
her eyes like twinkling lotus blossoms.

In this chest from pirate ships,
she finds not only jewels and coins.
She finds a princess crown replete,
with dark red rubies and complete,
with emeralds glowing bright and neat.

She takes the crown and swims away,
thinks of the daughter of a sailor,
lost at sea, not to return,
his ship a ten-ton sturdy whaler.

This crown she holds is for the maiden,
a little princess of the mainland,
and that is where this crown will rest,
on golden curls and neatly pressed.

The Mermaid *Maciella* and the Deep Velvet Coral

As velvet as the midnight sky,
bright coral grows in rows divine,
at a place where sea meets shore,
and forms an intricate design.

In caverns deep along the ledge,
where cattails settle on the edge,
the shore is filled with starfish bathing,
like golden suns, bright, breathtaking.

And at this place where sea meets shore,
the velvet coral is hidden deep
by conch shells scattered wide and far,
as dark as any sailor's sleep.

But *Maciella* knows the legend,
knows where the velvet coral grows,
underneath the purple conch shells,
concealing pearls in rows and rows.

These pearls, a silky turquoise blue,
legends tell were made for queens,
for mermaids of the seven seas,
their beauty hidden and unseen.

Below the waves in waters clear,
she plucks the pearls one by one.
Her conch shell full, she swims to moonlight,
her heartfelt duty all but done.
And soon these shiny, twinkling pearls
will rest in needy, thankful hands,
of her sailor lover's daughter,
a solitary, lovely maiden,
who dwells among the reeds and sands.

Her name is also *Maciella*,
or so the silent legend goes.
So, as she swims with sparkling pearls,
the love within her heart does grow.

The Mermaid *Queenella* and the Ship Without a Crew

Queenella has bright crimson fins,
as bright as glowing, rising suns.
They sparkle in the moonlight dim,
angelic bright, like praying nuns.

Her crimson fins do mesmerize,
entice red snappers by her side,
as they swim in silent rhythm
with the gently flowing tide.

From up above, a sea of red
floats upon a placid sea,
but the snappers know the way
to where the sunken ship rests free.

It is there *Queenella* dives,
below the pounding surf and waves,
to find the ship without a crew,
to find the sailors in their graves.

And when she finds the sunken hulk,
red snappers at her side,
she deftly swims and makes her way,
through open portholes, then inside.

The ship is empty, through and through,

no sailor, fish, or jewel in sight.
Just an empty, sunken ship,
with mysteries the sea holds tight.

But then a snapper, red as blood,
nudges her to search once more,
and through the murky, hollow depths,
they enter through a cabin door.

And there tied to a velvet pouch,
upon a coat rack dark and worn,
she finds a velvet scarf attached,
on it *Queenella* neatly drawn.

She clutches it with heartfelt tears,
red snappers at her side,
and swims to moonlight with the pouch,
and wonders what's inside.

In the soft light of the moon,
Queenella opens up the pouch.
In it rests her sailor love's
picture, as she feels his touch,
holds her breath, holds back her tears,
and yearns for lovestruck bygone years.

The Mermaid *Amara* and the Pirate's Cove

At a place along the shore,
where starfish swim in swirls and swirls,
Amara glides along the waves,
with silver fins and silver curls.

Schools of silver dollar fish
guide her to the place she seeks,
below the gently flowing waves,
along a bright blue coral reef.

Behind this reef a cove does rest,
a pirate's cove the legend tells.
It is there that treasure chests
are buried under turtles' shells.

The fish the color of her curls
find the place and swim in swirls,
and beneath their silky foam,
upon a chest, a silver comb,
as bright as any polished diamond,
rests alone just like an island.

Amara grasps the silver comb,
its handle shaped just like a key.
Into the chest it neatly fits.
She then unlocks a potpourri

of gold doubloons and yellow pearls,
of crosses silver, like her curls.

As she swims up to the surface,
a chain that holds a silver cross,
does adorn her neck so slender,
sparkling bright, her smile tender,
and glowing with a silver gloss.

The silver dollar fish so near,
now have swum to sunsets past,
as *Amara* seeks the mainland,
and her sailor love at last.

But he has sailed to far off lands,
while his daughter lingers still.
She plays among the reeds and sands,
and waits with gentle outstretched hands.

Amara does fulfill her duty,
calling out her maiden name,
Amara, just like hers, the same,
the silver necklace laid with reverence
upon the shore, her eyes aflame,
as young *Amara* the gift does claim.

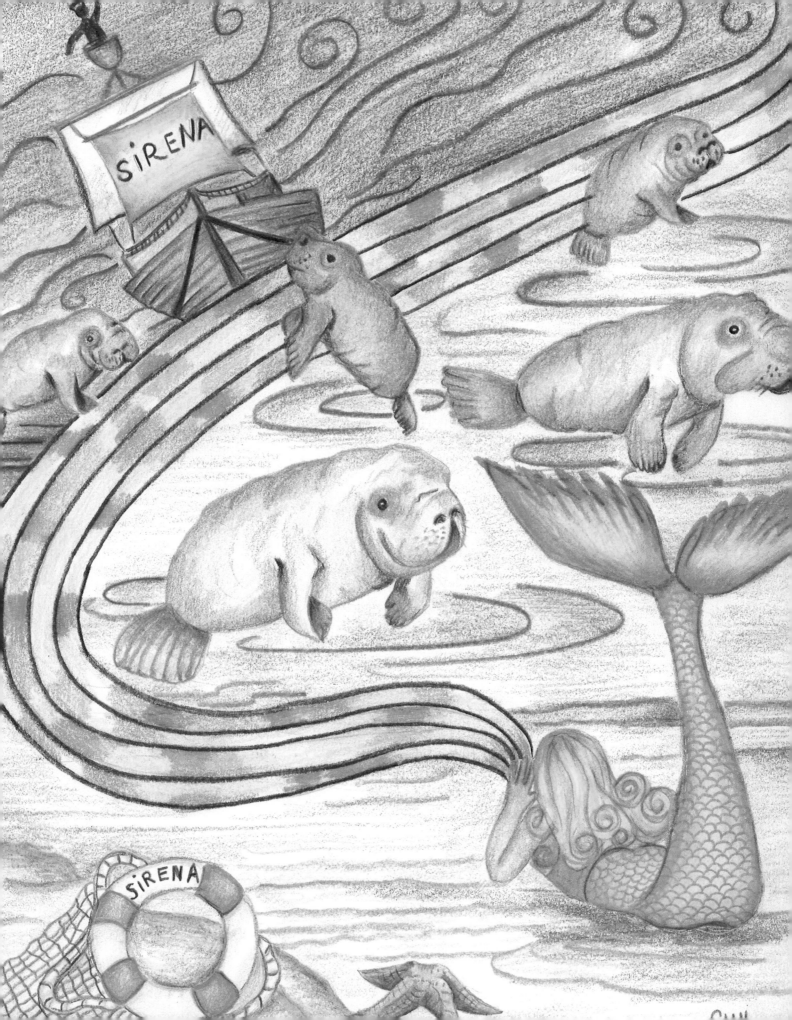

The Mermaid *Sirena* and the
Ship with the Golden Sail

Sirena, with her golden tail,
pursues a ship with a golden sail.
It sails alone on rumbling seas,
through driving rains and sailors' pleas.

Upon this ship her sailor love
sits within the crow's nest high,
waiting for *Sirena's* song,
with a wary seaman's eye.

The waves are steep, the ocean deep,
and sparkling blue like sapphire rings.
Sirena sings her mermaid song.
The sailor to the rail does cling.

The ship has many flowing sails
but only one is gold,
an ensign in the crow's nest high,
and in the wind it does unfold.

And on it clear in seaman's script,
Sirena's name displayed,
it flutters in the wind unfurled,
above the rolling, rocking waves.

A tempest from the deep, dark west
approaches recklessly.
Sirena sings her maiden song,
summoning a manatee.

This manatee, blue gray his colors,
leads a school a thousand thick,
and with their swishing, blue gray tails,
provides safe passage for the ship.

The golden ensign high above,
does wave and dance unscathed,
and with his hand upon his lips,
her sailor lover gently waves.

The Mermaid *Stormi* and the Sea of a Thousand Tempests

Some seas are placid. Some are rough,
and *Stormi* knows them all.
Across the oceans wide and deep,
with sailing ships both large and small,
across the seas with rolling waves,
above the caverns and the caves,
and with her school of flying fish,
their lucent tails and fins do swish,
Stormi with her mermaid calls
protects from tempests and from squalls.

And when the flying fish do call,
above the waters fast and steep,
she hurries to their beck and call,
for they are guardians of the deep.

The blue and dark green waves they ride,
and with their vibrant wings they glide,
to help those stranded and in need,
relentless with resolve and speed.

Into a sea of hail and storms,
a thousand tempests wait,
and with her flying fish as guides,
into the raging storms she glides.

The lightening and the thunder thick,
the raindrops hard, as hard as bricks,
upon her school of flying fish
Stormi rides upon her knees,
and with her sweet and solemn pleas,
they grant her heartfelt wish.

With their thousand slashing tails,
with their thousand flapping wings,
the storm abates and on the ships
the sails unfurl in friendly winds.

And as these ships sail to the west,
the tempests out of sight,
Stormi and her flying fish,
disappear into the night.

The Mermaid *Tifara* and the Stranded Clipper

The clipper floats on dead calm seas,
no wind in sight, just shallow breeze,
and with the heat from cloudless skies,
saltwater drips from sailors' eyes.

The ensign in the crow's nest waves.
It flutters in the dwindling breeze,
but *Tifara* knows the ship,
and feels the sailors' silent pleas.

In blue-green seas, both flat and calm,
on the edge she holds her palm,
and with her sweet and calming tone,
she calls their names and waits alone.

They soon arrive in thickened schools,
gray dolphins with their slashing tails.
Tifara leads them to the ship.

They soon are joined by blue-black whales.

The whales and dolphins listen low,
as *Tifara*, eyes aglow,
urges them to push the ship,
steady, neatly, not too slow,
into the wind not far away,
and from the doldrums dark and gray.

In time the sails gather wind.
The clipper ship is underway.
The dolphins gather by her side.
The whales have swum far, far away.

And as the slowly rising sun,
signals that her work is done,
Tifara to her dolphin friends,
blows a kiss. The journey ends.

The Mermaid *Arista* and the Moonless Night

Some nights are bright with colored moons,
that glow with moonbeams like the stars.
Other nights are dark and deep,
above the waters, dark and steep.

Arista, with her moonbeam eyes,
scans the oceans and the skies,
for wayward ships gone astray,
for sailors lost along the way.

She rides a seahorse brightly red,
and gently, slowly pats his head,
urges him to scan the waters,
looking for lost sons and daughters.

At their sides are lantern fish.
They glow in deepest, darkest night.
Their eyes, a lovely deep-set blue,
their scales glow with a velvet hue.

And on a moonless, starless night,
with shiny scales and glistening light,
these lantern fish make out a form,
a clipper ship lost in a storm.

Motionless, it waits for aid.
Its sails are tattered, ripped, and torn.
It lists to starboard, floating free,
among the damage from the storm.

Seven sailors wait on deck,
seven sailors only.
Waving frantically they call,
seaman's whistles one and all.

Arista knows their frantic calls,
knows the sailors one by one,
whispers to the lantern fish,
what is needed to be done.

In minutes they are there in schools,
porpoises both sleek and long.
With bobbing heads above the water,
they listen to her maiden song.

Upon their arched and dark, gray backs,
seven sailors soon do ride.
Across the blue-green ocean waves,
and to the mainland they do glide.

The Mermaid *Cariana* and the Sailfish with the Sapphire Fin

The sleek and darting sailfish,
all colored brightly blue,
swim in pairs among the waves.
They swim in tandem two by two.

But *Cariana* knows full well
when danger is in sight.
The sailfish with the sapphire fin
will guide her through the restless night.

A tempest forming in the west,
surrounded by dark, swirling winds,
brings the sailfish to her side.
His sapphire fin will be her guide.

The other sailfish come in pairs,

their fins a lighter hue.
But only one, upon his back,
has a fin of sapphire blue.

As the tempest rages near,
as the waves unfold in sheets,
the sailfish with the sapphire fin,
leads them through the rain and sleet.

And from the dark, black coal-like skies,
the mermaid *Cariana's* eyes,
as bright as topaz in the hail,
just like her guiding sapphire sail,
does emerge unscathed and safe,
from thunder, pelting rain and din.
She follows close the sapphire fin.

The Mermaid *Mariella* and the Yellow Tang Fish

As bright as any golden coins,
the yellow tang fish swim in schools.
Along a beach with ivory sands,
they come and wait near swirling pools,
as *Mariella* claps her hands.

On a rock ledge green with moss,
Mariella calls their names.
Two by two they swim in tandem,
two by two, their movements random,
as their scales do glow and glisten,
like a dazzling golden ransom.

The little mermaids watch and listen,
as *Mariella* her song does sing.
The yellow tang fish, fins that glisten,
swim along the shore and bring
their lovely, golden, vibrant colors,
like a sparkling golden ring.

The lesson done, these little mermaids,
their tails all swishing with delight,
and to the yellow tang fish fins,
they hold them firm and ever tight,
as they swim through foam and waves,
in friendly waters, above sea caves.

The Mermaid *Aliana* and the Ten Little Mermaids

The ten little mermaids,
on ten spunky seahorses,
listened as *Aliana*
began teaching the courses.

The first course she taught
was how to ride slow.
The next course she taught
was how to *giddy-up-and-go.*

So ten little mermaids,
with long, auburn curls,

on ten spunky seahorses,
rode through waves and sea swirls.

So all through the day
and deep into the night
the ten little mermaids
on their steeds they held tight.

And when it was over,
and when it was done
the ten little mermaids
were all having fun.

The Mermaid *Yasmina* and the Empty Lighthouse

Above the sea, on a ledge of stone,
the lighthouse stood quite all alone.
No sailor lived there. No mariner dared.
The lightening flashed. Winds howled and blared,
but most of all, the tempests flared.

But then one day before a storm,
a sailor arrived, his job to perform.
All alone he was, except for his cat.
On his head was an old green mariner's hat.

His cat was the color of matted up hay.
Yasmina knew not how long they would stay.
With the winds and the rain,
and the pelting cold hail,
no sailor remained.
No mariner prevailed.

But *Yasmina* did swim in the waters nearby.
She guarded the lighthouse, watched ever the sky,
for tempests and storms, for winds low and high,
for squalls and for rain, and to warn whomever
all alone in the lighthouse remained.

And then one day
in the frosty, cold mist,
along the steep shore

the waves seldom kissed,
the sailor and cat,
saw her swimming alone.
So, he tipped his green hat,
his hair wispy and blown.

With a grin on his face,
he blew her a kiss.
The cat with its tail
saw nothing amiss,
and swished it with ease
in the soft sea-salt breeze.

She held up her conch,
green-white were its colors,
and from her sweet lips
he soon did discover
her sweet mermaid chant,
and unlike any other.

"In case there is danger,"
she said, breathing lightly.
"I see," said the sailor,
his cap tipped politely.

So, back into the sea
Yasmina did swim,
looked back at the sailor,
blew a kiss back toward him.

The Mermaid *Barbiana* and the Silver Unicorn

On a narrow beach lined with cattails and reeds,
a unicorn roamed wearing bright colored beads.
The beads were the color of deep oceans blue,
of coral and seashells, shiny and new,
but the unicorn's horn had a deep silver hue.

Barbiana did swim along the cattails and reeds,
along the shore that was littered with rushes
and weeds.
The waters were shallow but clear as a bell,
and a place where the silver unicorn dwelled.

He galloped quite freely throughout the long day,

his beads like a rainbow, a vibrant array.
Barbiana swam freely from morning 'til night,
her bright silver beads a glorious sight.

And then one day on that sandy white beach,
eye to eye, their curious glances did meet,
and when it was over and when it was done,
a rainbow of beads did flash in the sun,
from *Barbiana's* slim neck, while her bright
silver beads,
on the unicorn glowed through the rushes and
reeds.

The Mermaid *Cypriana* and the Frogs on the Beach

The beach was surrounded by marshes and bogs.
It was simply the home of a thousand red frogs.
Throughout most of the day they croaked out their tunes,
that lasted quite long into late afternoons.

They sat on old stumps and old rotting logs.
Their sweet bullfrog cadence covered the bogs.
But when it got dark a large bulbous bullfrog
began croaking quite loudly as he sat on a log.

So *Cypriana* through the misty twilight,
to the beach did return in the soft, dwindling light,

and there on the log sat the rather large frog,
as he continued his croaking through the marshes and bogs.

And when he saw *Cypriana*, he jumped rather high.
He almost jumped as high as the sky,
and when he returned, on the log he did land,
surrounded by a thousand red frogs like a band,
as the croaking increased and covered the bogs,
while a thousand red frogs on a thousand old logs,
croaked out their sweet tunes through the marshes and bogs.

The Mermaid *Dulciana:* The Lantern in the Night

Dulciana, the mermaid, swam alone in the night,
beginning in the glowing and twinkling twilight.
Along white sandy beaches and white coral reefs,
among rushes and reeds, and floating brown leaves,
among overgrown weeds and cattails quite tall,
scanning the waves and the waters for any and all
creatures in need, whether large or quite small,
and for any lost sailors who heeded her call.

By her side were two lantern fish, shining like candles.
Bright blue were their scales aglow in the night.
On her seahorse, bright red, appearing like handles,
were two glowing eels to which she held tight.

These colors were signals to lost, stranded sailors
that *Dulciana* was near and would soon aid their plight.
The eels glowed brightly with gold flickering colors
when *Dulciana* released them into the night.

And so night after night *Dulciana* did search,
in the quiet of the night like an old sailor's church,
aiding lost mermaids in dark, dangerous waters,
rescuing fathers, mothers, and daughters,
and sons who were sailors lost in dark storms,
and rescuing fish in schools and large swarms.
She rescued sea creatures lost in the night.
She searched and she searched in the twinkling moonlight.

The Mermaid *Harmony* and the Little Lost Mermaid

The little lost mermaid was not to be found.
So, the octopus named *Orchid* looked all around.
She looked and she looked but nothing was found.
She then told sweet *Harmony*, whose skills were renowned,
to search, and to search, until she was found.

So, the mermaid sweet *Harmony*,
with long reddish curls,
followed her sting ray
through sea swells and swirls.

She knew all the waters, the marshes, and bogs.
She knew all the beaches where lived all the frogs.
She knew the thick rushes, the tall growing reeds.
So, she searched through the cattails, the caves, and the weeds.

She searched through the caverns, deep under the water.
She searched and she searched like *Orchid* had taught her.

And late that night on a rock near the shore,
the little lost mermaid, lost not anymore,
her eyes sparkling like gems, like shiny blue pearls,
and her silky, smooth hair with curl after curl,
and her hair like white coral with her fins deeply green,
she sang out her song with a smile quite serene.

She held in her hand, among the cattails and reeds,
a singular flower across her green knees,
as the frogs and the toads perched on large lily pads,
croaked out their sweet tunes, *Harmony* no longer sad.

The Mermaid *Evelina* and the
Sailor with the Pelican

On a beach with starfish gleaming,
her orange-red hair is flashing, streaming,
as his clipper ship makes way,
into the sun-streaked, golden bay.

Her fins are blue as amethysts.
Her harp is golden like the sun.
Her eyes wide-open as she waits,
she counts the seconds one by one.

His hat is blue with scarlet trim.
She whistles out her song to him,

and on the water, streaking gold,
foretells a mermaid legend old,
of a sailor lost at sea,
a long-lost sailor, brave and bold
returning to his mermaid love,
the golden sunset high above.

In the crow's nest on his ship,
her sailor love does blow a kiss,
as *Evelina* strums her harp,
ever soft and, oh, so sweet,
a long-beaked pelican at his feet.